Original title:
Crystalline Echoes

Author: Liina Liblikas
ISBN HARDBACK: 978-9916-79-966-6
ISBN PAPERBACK: 978-9916-79-967-3
ISBN EBOOK: 978-9916-79-968-0

Radiance Unfolding

In the dawn's soft embrace,
Golden beams begin to rise,
Whispers from the silent trees,
Carried on the morning sighs.

Each petal holds a secret,
In shades of blush, they confide,
Nature’s canvas painted bright,
With colors that never hide.

The rivers dance with sunlight,
Glittering on rocks so old,
Liquid gems in motion swift,
Their stories waiting to be told.

Clouds drift like feathered dreams,
Painting skies in hues of grey,
Yet behind those veils of mist,
Radiance yearns to find its way.

Nightfall brings its tapestry,
Of stars like thoughts in the mind,
In the whispers of the dark,
A brighter world you’ll surely find.

Celestial Chimes

In the silence of the night,
Stars begin their gentle dance,
They sing to the waiting hearts,
In a cosmic, timeless trance.

Moonlight spills like silver threads,
Weaving through the dreams we chase,
Echoes of forgotten songs,
In the vast, enchanted space.

Galaxies spin their stories,
Of love and loss intertwined,
Each twinkle holds a promise,
Of warmth for the heart and mind.

Comets blaze with fiery tails,
Drawing maps across the sky,
Telling tales of ancient times,
As we stand and wonder why.

In the symphony of night,
The universe hums along,
Every note a whispered wish,
In the heart, we find our song.

The Poetry of Light

Light breaks softly through the trees,
A gentle hand upon the ground,
Guiding dreams with tender grace,
In the silence, truth is found.

Every ray a poem bright,
Weaving through the shades of green,
Nature speaks in vibrant hues,
Painting worlds that might have been.

Sunset drapes the heavens wide,
In ribbons of crimson and gold,
A masterpiece unfolding slow,
As the evening tales are told.

Candles flicker in the dark,
Dancing shadows on the wall,
Each flame a verse of hope and love,
In their glow, we feel it all.

The dawn will come again, anew,
With promises that softly ignite,
In the rhythm of our days,
We write the poetry of light.

The Mirage of Clarity

In the desert of the mind, bright rays,
Illusions dance, lost in the haze.
Thoughts drift like sand in the breeze,
Seeking truth amongst the trees.

A hidden spring just out of sight,
Teasing shadows in the light.
With each step, the vision fades,
Leaving dreams in quiet glades.

Waves of doubt crash on the shore,
Promises made, yet nothing more.
Each glimmer calls, yet feels so far,
A flicker lost, a distant star.

The heart yearns for a guiding hand,
To navigate this shifting sand.
Yet here we stand, trapped in place,
Chasing visions in endless space.

In the mirage, we find our peace,
A fleeting moment that will cease.
For clarity is but a game,
A spark that flickers, then is tame.

Veils of Luminescence

Beneath the stars, a shimmering veil,
Whispers of light tell a tale.
Softly glowing, like sunrise hue,
A world transformed, bright and new.

Through the darkness, colors play,
Dancing shadows lead the way.
With every step, the night unfolds,
A tapestry of stories told.

Glimmers weave through the air,
Casting dreams, so light and rare.
Each flicker a promise, a breath,
Life in layers, in and out of death.

The moonlight drapes, a silver thread,
Binding moments, glory spread.
In this space where hopes align,
Veils of luminescence twine.

As dawn approaches, shadows fade,
Yet memories in light are made.
In the afterglow, we find our way,
Veils of luminescence will stay.

Echoes in the Crystal Chamber

Within the dome of crystal bright,
Echoes dance in silent night.
Whispers carried through the glass,
Memories that flicker, pass.

Footsteps soft on polished floor,
Tales of fortune, dreams of yore.
Each reflection, a story spun,
A world reborn, yet still undone.

Fragments of laughter, tears of joy,
Timeless tales of girl and boy.
In the chamber, feelings swell,
A sacred space, a woven spell.

Sunlight filters, colors blend,
Old regrets begin to mend.
The echoes whisper, soft refrain,
Calling us to rise again.

In the crystal, truth resides,
A sanctuary where hope abides.
With every sound, we start anew,
Echoes guide us, ever true.

Shattered Reflections

In shards of glass, the past is seen,
Broken dreams and what has been.
Memories carve into the air,
Fragile whispers of despair.

Each fragment tells a tale untold,
Of love and loss, of courage bold.
A portrait splintered, colors clash,
Life’s tapestry, torn in a flash.

Yet in the chaos, light may seep,
Healing softly, from the deep.
Through cracks that mar the perfect view,
Beauty rises, fierce and true.

In shattered pieces, we perceive,
A deeper truth in what we grieve.
For brokenness can lead to grace,
In every cut, a sacred space.

From the shards, we learn to soar,
Finding strength we can explore.
Reflections change, yet still we stand,
In shattered beauty, hand in hand.

Whispered Fragments

In memories we softly tread,
Where whispers dance and secrets spread.
Each fragment glows like fading light,
A tapestry of day and night.

In shadows cast from distant dreams,
The world unravels at the seams.
With every breath, we find our way,
In whispered words, we long to stay.

Through tangled paths of thought and time,
We weave our tales with silent rhyme.
Emotions surge, a gentle stream,
In every fragment, lies a dream.

Fragments whisper, softly heard,
In silent beats, the heart's own word.
The nightingale sings, so sweetly near,
In whispered fragments, love appears.

Each moment caught in tender sighs,
Like fleeting birds that touch the skies.
Embracing echoes, we will find,
The whispered fragments of the mind.

Luminous Resonance

In twilight's glow, the stars ignite,
A resonance that feels so right.
Each glimmer sings a tender tune,
As shadows merge with silver moon.

Waves of color spill like dreams,
In vibrant bursts, the daylight beams.
A symphony of light takes flight,
In every pulse, a world so bright.

Echoes linger, soft and clear,
Each wave a whisper, close and near.
In radiant hues, our hearts align,
A luminous dance, you’re truly mine.

Moments captured, fleeting spark,
In resonances, we leave our mark.
Together, we create the sound,
In this soft light, our love unbound.

With every heartbeat, colors blend,
In vivid strokes, our spirits mend.
A canvas painted with love's grace,
In luminous resonance, we find our place.

Glacial Reverberations

In icy realms where silence reigns,
A echoed hum in crystal chains.
With every breath, the frost takes flight,
As winter whispers, cold and bright.

Beneath the snow, a heart can beat,
In glacial depths, the dreamers meet.
Each layer thick with time’s embrace,
Reflecting light, a solemn grace.

Reverberations, soft yet clear,
In frozen worlds, we hold so dear.
A harmony of chill and cheer,
In glacial whispers, we draw near.

The mountains cradle ancient tales,
In every flake, a story pales.
With time slipping, we forge the bond,
In reverberations, our love responds.

The winds will sing, the ice will sigh,
Through glacial realms, together we fly.
In timeless echoes, we remain,
In glacial reverberations, love's refrain.

Prismatic Murmurs

In rain's embrace, the colors swirl,
A prismatic dance begins to twirl.
Each drop a note in nature’s song,
In murmurs sweet, we drift along.

Fragments of light through prisms chase,
Creating joy in every space.
With every hue, a new delight,
In vibrant whispers, hearts unite.

The world ignites with fleeting dreams,
In prismatic beams, our laughter gleams.
Each moment catches, bright and bold,
A story spun in colors told.

Murmurs rise from earth and sky,
In every breath, we laugh and cry.
Together woven, threads of fate,
In prismatic whispers, we create.

With open hearts and eyes that see,
The beauty wrapped in you and me.
In every shade, a truth discovered,
In prismatic murmurs, we are covered.

Ethereal Resonance

In shadows soft, whispers roam,
A dance of light, where spirits comb.
The air is thick with dreams unspoken,
In silent notes, the heart is broken.

Reflections pulse like echoes clear,
Each breath a hymn, both far and near.
Through veils of mist, we drift and sway,
In realms of dusk, we lose our way.

The world retreats, we fly as one,
Beneath the stars, till night is done.
With every beat, a tether formed,
In ethereal threads, our souls are warmed.

A Symphony of Shards

Glass pieces shimmer, under moonlight,
Fragments of stories, lost in the night.
Each shard a note, a tale to unveil,
Composing the silence, where echoes prevail.

In this mosaic, a haunting refrain,
Notes dance together, through pleasure and pain.
They rise and they fall, in a tempestuous tide,
A symphony born from what others hide.

The harmony built from fractured past,
Crafting a song that's meant to last.
As broken hearts learn to croon,
In a world that whispers, to the brightening moon.

Dancing with Transparency

Veils of clarity, drape the night,
In the midst of shadows, we find our light.
With every step, a ripple flows,
As we twirl and spin, the secret glows.

The truth unveils in the softest sway,
Each movement a whisper, guiding the way.
We marvel at visions, impossible dreams,
In the fabric of air, reality seems.

Our souls entwined, in the gentle grace,
Finding freedom, in this sacred space.
Through glass-like hearts, we dance anew,
In moments of pure, translucent hue.

Melodies of the Shattered

From broken silence, music flows,
In jagged notes, the beauty grows.
Each fracture tells of stories deep,
Awakening spirits from their sleep.

We gather pieces, lost and found,
Crafting a chorus, a hopeful sound.
In the dance of chaos, we find our way,
The shattered echoes, refuse to sway.

With every heartbeat, a fracture sings,
In the tapestry woven from our wings.
We embrace the shards, their glimmering art,
In melodies deep, we mend the heart.

Glistening Whispers

Moonlight dances on the sea,
Whispers carry wild and free.
Stars are secrets in the night,
Glistening dreams take fragile flight.

Leaves of silver sway and glide,
Nature's breath, a soft confide.
Echoes sing through twilight's veil,
Glistening truths in every tale.

Waves enchant with gentle hush,
In the stillness, hearts will rush.
Murmurs wrapped in night's embrace,
Glistening whispers fill the space.

Through the dark, a lantern shines,
Guided by the soft divines.
In each flicker, hope is found,
Glistening tales that astound.

As dawn breaks, the whispers fade,
Promises in light displayed.
Yet in shadows, memories lie,
Glistening whispers never die.

Frozen Echoes

In winter's chill, the world stands still,
Frozen echoes, time to kill.
Snowflakes fall with silent grace,
Whispers caught in a white embrace.

Crystals form on branches bare,
Nature's art, a frosty flare.
Each soft sigh, a moment caught,
Frozen echoes, a dream wrought.

Footprints trace the paths we made,
In the silence, memories played.
Echoes linger, soft and long,
Frozen whispers, a haunting song.

Stillness reigns in the pale light,
Frozen echoes of day and night.
In the heart, a warmth survives,
Echoes frozen, yet love thrives.

As spring approaches, time will thaw,
Echoes fade, but love's the law.
In the glimmer of life's return,
Frozen echoes, forever burn.

Prismatic Dreams

Colors swirl in vibrant dance,
Prismatic dreams, a fleeting chance.
Rainbows arch above the skies,
Every hue, a sweet surprise.

Through the prism, visions shine,
Fragments twirl, a tale divine.
In each shade, a whisper speaks,
Prismatic dreams, the heart it seeks.

In twilight's glow, the world ablaze,
Painting shadows in a haze.
Dreams unfold in dazzling light,
Prismatic wonders, pure delight.

Through the window, colors blend,
Life is art that has no end.
In the soul, these dreams take flight,
Prismatic visions, shining bright.

As daylight fades to evening's hue,
Dreams awake in colors new.
In the dark, they brightly gleam,
Prismatic wishes, endless dream.

Echoes of Light

In the dawn, the shadows flee,
Echoes of light, wild and free.
Sunrise paints the world aglow,
Whispers of warmth in every flow.

Golden rays break through the dark,
Layers of hope ignite a spark.
In the silence, dreams ignite,
Echoes of light, a pure delight.

Candles flicker, softly swayed,
Guiding thoughts that won't evade.
In each flicker, stories share,
Echoes of light in the air.

Moments captured, fleeting fast,
Echoes linger from the past.
In our hearts, their warmth will stay,
Echoes of light, come what may.

As night falls, the stars will weave,
Tales of light, we will believe.
In the cosmos, dreams take flight,
Whispers echo, pure and bright.

When Light Becomes Sound

In the dawn, whispers weave,
Colors ripple, softly breathe.
A symphony, bright and pure,
Silent songs begin to lure.

Echoes dance on golden rays,
Harmony in sunlit ways.
Radiance breaks the quiet night,
Transforming dark to purest light.

Cascading tones, a gentle breeze,
Notes of warmth, they come to tease.
Drifting softly, as they play,
Guiding shadows on their way.

Illuminated melodies rise,
Crown the world in sweet disguise.
As the day unfolds its hue,
Light and sound embrace anew.

In the twilight, colors fade,
Yet the echoes will not trade.
Transience in every sound,
When light bursts forth, all is found.

Resplendent Murmurs

Whispers brushing through the trees,
Nature sings with rugged ease.
Sunbeams filter, soft and bright,
All around, the world feels right.

Glistening leaves in soft repose,
Gentle laughter, breezy flows.
Through the branches, secrets play,
In the twilight, night holds sway.

Fleeting shadows pass us by,
Echoes linger in the sky.
Rustling dreams and fading light,
Murmurs blend with coming night.

Shimmering stars, a silent choir,
Filling hearts with soft desire.
Every shimmer, a story told,
Resplendent joy in hues of gold.

Rustling echoes, whispers blend,
All around, the night extends.
Melodies of a tranquil land,
In resplendent murmurs, we stand.

Prisms of Solitude

In a room where shadows dwell,
Quiet thoughts begin to swell.
Colors fracture, light refracts,
In this peace, time slowly cracks.

Every corner, secrets hide,
Whispers in the heart, they bide.
Fractured beams of inner light,
Guide the soul through endless night.

Lonely echoes, soft and low,
In their stillness, wisdom grows.
A prism's tale, a thought so deep,
In solitude, the heart will leap.

Fragments swirl, a quiet stream,
Turning silence into dream.
Each reflection, a silent part,
Of the journey through the heart.

In these prisms, we find hope,
A gentle way for souls to cope.
Each hue a name, each shade a sound,
In solitude, we are unbound.

Chimes of the Unseen

In the meadow, bells resound,
Echoes linger all around.
Softly calling, breezes play,
Chimes of wonder greet the day.

Spirit whispers through the air,
Unseen presences linger there.
All the magic wrapped in sound,
In each note, the heart is found.

Fragments of a forgotten song,
Carried where the lost belong.
Every chime, a tale unfolds,
Telling secrets, centuries old.

In the silence, voices thrive,
Hidden tunes that come alive.
Life in rhythm, gently sways,
Chimes of dusk in twilight days.

Let the echoes guide the way,
To the dawn of a new day.
In the unseen's soft embrace,
Harmony finds its rightful place.

Weaving Through Glass

In shadows cast by light, we tread,
Fractured visions dance ahead.
A tapestry of dreams held tight,
Stitched together in the night.

Each glimmer sparkles, hopes entwine,
Reflections hold a touch divine.
Through glass and grace, we find our way,
In every shimmer, the heart will sway.

Fleeting moments, fragments play,
Time's soft hand leads us astray.
Yet amidst the shards, we create bliss,
A harmony that none can dismiss.

So let us weave with care and might,
Through crystal paths, we'll chase the light.
In every layer, lives a tale,
A whispered dream that will prevail.

Crystalized Whispers

In frosty air, the secrets dwell,
Softly sung, a silent spell.
Beneath the ice, a world concealed,
Whispers linger, dreams revealed.

Shattering silence with each breath,
Echoes dance, defying death.
Crystalized moments whisper low,
A symphony of tales to flow.

Glistening paths in winter's grasp,
Hold our hopes in tender clasp.
Through chilly winds, we find our song,
Where every heartbeat guides us along.

Embrace the frost, the frozen dew,
In fragile forms, love shines anew.
Together we weave, through time we bend,
In crystal whispers, we ascend.

The Harmony of Stillness

In tranquil dawn, the world holds breath,
Whispers float beyond the depth.
Serenity in each soft gust,
Moments held, in peace we trust.

A forest dense, the silence speaks,
In nature's arms, our solace peaks.
Still waters mirror skies above,
Reflecting dreams, a realm of love.

Time slows down, as shadows blend,
In quietude, our hearts ascend.
With each heartbeat, stillness grows,
A gentle rush where calmness flows.

So breathe the air, embrace the space,
In harmony, find your place.
Let stillness guide your weary soul,
In quiet moments, become whole.

Shards of Serenity

In fragments bright, the calm resides,
Shattered peace where beauty hides.
Each shard reflects a different hue,
A mosaic crafted just for you.

Through scattered light, we forge a path,
From broken pieces, rise from wrath.
In every sliver, hope is found,
A symphony within the sound.

Embrace the cracks, the flaws we share,
In imperfections, love lays bare.
Whispers call from every seam,
In shattered forms, we craft a dream.

So gather close, the fragments bright,
In unity, we find our light.
With shards of grace, we will repair,
Creating beauty, beyond compare.

Snowy Soundscapes

Whispers of snow fall down,
Covering the earth like a crown.
Footsteps soft on frozen ground,
A hush envelops all around.

Pine trees wear their coats of white,
Underneath the pale moonlight.
Nature's symphony unfolds,
In the beauty winter holds.

Icicles hang from rooftops high,
Glistening like stars in the sky.
A breath of frost, a gentle sigh,
In this snow, our spirits fly.

Children laugh, their voices cheer,
Building snowmen, spreading cheer.
The world transformed, a wondrous sight,
Drifting dreams in purest white.

As twilight fades, the shadows creep,
The night descends, the world is deep.
In snowy soundscapes, peace resides,
Where winter's grace forever hides.

The Resounding Stillness

In the silent woods, I tread,
Every whisper fills my head.
Leaves that murmur, rustle, sway,
Echoes of the fading day.

The brook sings low, a gentle call,
Among the trees, a soft enthrall.
Clouds drift by in shades of gray,
As night prepares to take the day.

Stars awaken, twinkling bright,
Casting dreams in silver light.
Stillness wraps the earth in peace,
In this moment, worries cease.

Time stands still, the world in pause,
Nature's beauty, no need for applause.
A breath of calm, a tranquil mind,
In the resounding stillness, we unwind.

As shadows stretch and night descends,
We find solace, as the day ends.
In quietude, the heart finds rest,
A gentle lull, where we are blessed.

Pristine Echoes

Across the valley, echoes play,
In melodies of bright array.
Nature's chorus, pure and true,
Whispers softly, calling you.

Mountains rise with solemn grace,
Reflecting light in every space.
A song of earth, a serenade,
In pristine echoes, dreams are made.

Rivers flow with crystal cheer,
Carrying tales for those who hear.
The wind's caress, an airy flight,
Bringing stories of day and night.

Fields of flowers dance and sway,
In vibrant colors, bold display.
Together in this sacred place,
Pristine echoes, we embrace.

The sun dips low, the shadows play,
In twilight's glow, they drift away.
With every sound, our spirits soar,
In pristine echoes, we explore.

Mirage of Light

In the desert, the sun holds sway,
Casting shadows in a vibrant array.
Waves of heat rise, shimmer bright,
A mirage dances, pure delight.

Golden dunes stretch far and wide,
Where secrets of the sands abide.
The horizon bends, a mystic flight,
Illusions cloaked in morning light.

Whispers of wind through canyon walls,
Echoing softly as silence calls.
A fleeting vision, all takes flight,
Chasing dreams in the blinding light.

Stars emerge as dusk rolls in,
The world transforms, anew within.
A tapestry woven of day and night,
In every heartbeat, a mirage of light.

As dawn approaches, wonders gleam,
Painting the landscape, like a dream.
In this voyage, we find our sight,
Lost in the beauty, a mirage of light.

Translucent Murmurs

Whispers float through silver air,
Dreams are born from gentle care.
In shadows soft, the secrets lie,
Beneath the calm, the echoes sigh.

Each breath a tale, a silent song,
In twilight's grace, we all belong.
Moments brush the edge of night,
Translucent murmurs take their flight.

With every glance, the spirits play,
In the dance of night and day.
Melodies weave through the haze,
Guiding hearts in wondrous ways.

The world spins soft in twilight's glow,
Secrets blossoming as they flow.
In tender whispers, love awakes,
Translucent paths our journey makes.

The Clarity of Ice

Frozen still beneath the sun,
Moments shine where shadows run.
Through crystal paths, the vision flows,
In every shard, a story grows.

Reflections dance upon the ground,
In silent grace, they spin around.
The world refracted, clear and bright,
A fleeting glimpse of pure delight.

Yet with the warmth, the truth appears,
Melting edges, exposing fears.
But in the cold, a beauty lies,
In the clarity, no disguise.

Each droplet tells a tale of old,
Of icy hearts and flames bold.
In winter’s breath, the memories trace,
A world unveiled, a frozen grace.

Fractured Symphonies

Note by note, the chaos weaves,
In broken chords, the heart believes.
Within the clash, a song is born,
From shattered dreams, the spirit's worn.

In every scar, the echoes ring,
A fractured song, a vibrant thing.
The melodies of loss and gain,
In gilded notes, a hint of pain.

Among the shards, the harmonies rise,
Twisting through the midnight skies.
With every sound, a pulse takes flight,
Fractured symphonies of light.

So let the music flow and bend,
In every end, there lies a mend.
Through brokenness, a truth is found,
In whispered chords, the lost are crowned.

Radiant Fragments

Shattered glass in sunlight beams,
Radiant fragments spark the dreams.
Colors swirl in vibrant play,
Each piece reflects a sunlit ray.

In scattered hues, a tale unfolds,
Of stories past and futures bold.
With every glimmer, shadows fade,
Each fragment cherished, never strayed.

From chaos blooms a gorgeous view,
In every chip, a world anew.
Holding light in gentle sway,
Radiant fragments guide our way.

The beauty found in broken things,
In fractured dreams, the heart still sings.
Let us gather, piece by piece,
In radiant light, our souls find peace.

Chiming Glass

A soft breeze whispers lightly,
Through evenings dressed in gold,
Chimes of laughter linger,
Stories waiting to be told.

Ripples dance on surfaces,
Reflecting dreams aglow,
In the stillness, hearts collide,
With secrets soft and slow.

Colors blend in twilight,
Fragments of our past,
Echoes of our moments,
Wishing they would last.

In every clink, a promise,
In every breath, a sigh,
Time freezes in this magic,
Where memories never die.

The night unfolds in beauty,
As stars begin to play,
Chiming glass in harmony,
Carries us away.

Frosted Memories

Snowflakes fall like whispers,
Each one tells a tale,
In a world of frosted beauty,
Where every touch is frail.

Branches bend with burden,
Nature's crystal lace,
Hiding all our secrets,
In this chilly embrace.

Footprints mark our journey,
Woven into white,
Tracing back our laughter,
Chasing shadows of light.

Windows fog with warmth,
As memories entwine,
In a dance of time unbroken,
With love's tender design.

Each breath forms a story,
In the softest air,
Frosted memories linger,
With beauty, rich and rare.

The Sound of Clarity

A river flows in silence,
Whispers of the deep,
Secrets held in water,
In currents calm and steep.

Echoes drift like feathers,
Upon a breeze so light,
Carrying the wisdom,
Of shadows turning bright.

Moments pause in stillness,
In clarity we find,
Voices in the distance,
Revealing what's entwined.

In the hush of nature,
Every sound a guide,
Opening the pathways,
Where dreams and truth abide.

Resonance expands beyond,
Filling the vast space,
The sound of clarity sings,
In every heart's embrace.

Sparkling Silence

In the glow of twilight,
Stars begin to peek,
A canvas painted softly,
Where night and dreams do speak.

Silence drapes its shadow,
Caressing lonely hearts,
Yet deep within its stillness,
A spark of hope imparts.

Moments stretch and linger,
Embracing what is real,
In the folds of quiet,
We uncover how to heal.

Each breath becomes a story,
In the vastness of the night,
Securing all our wishes,
In the shimmering light.

Sparkling silence whispers,
A symphony of grace,
In the stillness, we discover,
A sacred, gentle space.

Frosted Echoes

Whispers of winter linger low,
On frosted paths where shadows grow.
Echoes of laughter, soft and bright,
Dance like snowflakes in pale twilight.

Moonlight glimmers on icy streams,
Painting the world in silver dreams.
Silent trees wear coats of white,
Guarding secrets of the night.

Footprints trace a fleeting sound,
In this realm where peace is found.
Echoing softly, time stands still,
In frosted echoes, hearts can fill.

With every breath, the chill draws near,
But amid the cold, warmth appears.
Embraced by nature's calm embrace,
We find our solace in this space.

So let the winter weave its tale,
Through frosty woods and frozen veil.
In echoes past, we find our song,
A melody where we belong.

Light's Silhouette

Shapes emerge in softest glow,
As daylight bids the night to flow.
Light casts shadows on the ground,
Whispers of dreams in silence found.

Colors blend in gentle hues,
Creating art the heart imbues.
Silhouettes sway with evening breeze,
Stories unfold with quiet ease.

Stars awaken, one by one,
Painting skies when day is done.
In the dusk, we sigh and breathe,
As light and dark begin to weave.

Every outline tells a tale,
In twilight's grasp, we gently sail.
Through the night, we wander slow,
In light's embrace, our spirits glow.

So let us dance in shadows cast,
Where time stands still, and moments last.
In every silhouette, we find,
A fleeting whisper for the mind.

Silent Glasswork

Fractured light through crystal frames,
Reflecting colors, whispering names.
In quiet halls where echoes play,
Silent glasswork adorns the day.

Glistening shapes in stillness lie,
Where dreams are caught, and hopes can fly.
Each shard a story, each piece a part,
Of art that speaks to the wandering heart.

With gentle care, the world unfolds,
In glassy realms where magic holds.
A prism caught in time's embrace,
Mirroring life with every trace.

Tales of wonder etched in light,
Crafting visions within the night.
In silence deep, we come to see,
The beauty born of artistry.

So let us marvel at the work,
Where shadows dance and secrets lurk.
In silent glass, our souls ignite,
Reflecting all the world's delight.

Frigid Melodies

Notes of winter fall like snow,
In crisp air where the cold winds blow.
Frigid melodies paint the sky,
As nature sings its lullaby.

Chilled whispers through the silent trees,
Carried softly on the breeze.
Each sound a tale, each note a thread,
Weaving warmth where hearts are led.

Frosty mornings greet the dawn,
While nightingale sings on the lawn.
In harmony with frosted grounds,
Music sparkles, joy abounds.

Echoing dreams of seasons past,
In frigid air, the spell is cast.
Through every chord, we find our way,
As time evolves both night and day.

So let the cold embrace your soul,
With frigid melodies that console.
In every note, find peace anew,
As winter's song sings just for you.

Faded Sparkles

Once bright, now dimmed light,
Threads of gold in the night,
Memories softly fade,
Chasing dreams long delayed.

Whispers of what was near,
Echoes that disappear,
Frost on petals lie,
Glimmers of days gone by.

In shadows, stories rest,
Hearts alone, unconfessed,
Stars twinkle from afar,
Lost in the evening's jar.

Time weaves its gentle art,
Crafting from dreams a part,
Yet in silence, we yearn,
For faded sparkles to return.

In twilight's tender glow,
Where the soft breezes flow,
Hope flickers like a flame,
Ever longing, just the same.

Luminous Lament

In shadows deep and wide,
Where sorrow seeks to hide,
A heart beats, heavy, slow,
Wishing for the light to show.

Ghostly whispers in the air,
Remembering love's sweet care,
Each tear, a star that falls,
A luminous voice that calls.

Through the night, we wander lost,
Bearing the heavy cost,
Of dreams that didn't last,
And futures locked in the past.

Yearning for hope's gentle spark,
In the silence, we embark,
To find solace in the pain,
A luminous path through the rain.

Yet in the mournful sighs,
A flicker never dies,
For even the darkest night,
Must yield to dawn's pure light.

Reflections in Still Waters

Mirrored skies on quiet lakes,
Soft currents as the heart wakes,
Ripples whisper to the trees,
Secrets shared with gentle ease.

In every glance, a story flows,
Captured time in tranquil prose,
Beneath the surface lies a dream,
A world untouched, a silver gleam.

Floating thoughts, a fleeting breeze,
Nature holds, calming seas,
Lost in echoes, lost in thought,
Life's reflections, gently caught.

Summoned by the evening light,
Shadows stretch to embrace night,
In the stillness, calm and deep,
A tranquil place, where secrets sleep.

So by this water's edge we stand,
Hopes and fears slip through our hands,
Yet in each splash, and every round,
Reflections of our souls abound.

Frost & Flame

A dance of frost upon the ground,
Beneath the sun, a warmth is found,
Contrasts twirl in the chill embraced,
Where fire and ice interlaced.

The crisp air bites but sparks ignite,
As winter fights with warm delight,
Glowing embers softly gleam,
In the heart of a frozen dream.

Silent whispers through the night,
Frozen fingers brush the light,
In this clash of shades extreme,
We find balance, dare to dream.

Frosty breaths and heated sighs,
Passions blaze, while still it lies,
In the interplay of seasons,
Love finds strength, despite the reasons.

Together they will twine and bend,
Frost and flame, they’ll never end,
In every shadow, every glow,
Life’s warmth in the cold will show.

Glimmers of the Heart

In shadows deep, where silence sleeps,
A flicker shines, a promise keeps.
Through tears that fall, like gentle rain,
Hope's soft glow soothes the pain.

With every breath, a spark ignites,
In darkest hours, the spirit fights.
Hearts entwined, in love's embrace,
Glimmers of joy, we must not chase.

The whispers sing, in twilight's hue,
Of dreams alive, and paths so true.
In quiet moments, solace found,
Glimmers of light, forever bound.

Through winding roads, our stories weave,
In each moment, we dare believe.
Together strong, we'll face the start,
For life is rich, with glimmers of heart.

Fragments of Light

In the canvas of night, stars gleam bright,
Each one a dream, a beacon of light.
Scattered across the vast, deep sky,
Whispers of hope that linger and fly.

With every dawn, a new chance born,
Fragments of light on the world's worn.
A tapestry woven, both fragile and bold,
Stories in colors, waiting to be told.

In quiet moments, reflections emerge,
Of paths we choose and dreams that surge.
The heart takes flight, on wings of grace,
Fragments of light, in every place.

Through valleys low and mountains high,
We gather the shards, and let them fly.
With hands outstretched, we reach for dreams,
Fragments of light, in endless streams.

Shattered Reflections

In cracked mirrors, truths unfold,
Fragments of stories, quietly told.
Through splintered glass, we see the past,
Shattered reflections, echoes that last.

The heart, a mosaic of love and pain,
In each broken piece, wisdom we gain.
Finding our way through shadows and light,
Shattered reflections, hinting at fight.

With every scar, a tale resides,
Of battles fought and dreams that bide.
In the depth of night, we learn to soar,
Shattered reflections, we rise once more.

Embracing the flaws that make us whole,
Each piece a journey, a glimpse of the soul.
Through fractured moments, we create art,
Shattered reflections, the beauty of heart.

Whispers in the Frost

A breath of winter, crisp and clear,
Whispers in the frost, secrets near.
Each icy crystal, a tale it bears,
Nature breathes softly, in quiet prayers.

Beneath the moon, shadows dance light,
Echoes of silence, a delicate sight.
In frozen stillness, the world feels small,
Whispers in the frost, a gentle call.

In swirling winds, stories are spun,
Of warmth to come, and battles won.
Embrace the chill, let worries cease,
Whispers in the frost, a promise of peace.

Through barren trees, a beauty lies,
In the heart of winter, hope never dies.
With every step, the world anew,
Whispers in the frost, guiding us through.

Radiant Memories

In the garden where we played,
Sunshine dances, dreams paraded.
Laughter lingers, sweet as honey,
Moments glowed, bright and sunny.

Days of gold, like pages turned,
In the heart, the fire burned.
Whispers soft, the breezes carry,
Tender scenes we often tarry.

Time like water flows away,
Yet in memories, we still stay.
Holding close the vibrant hues,
Painting life with every muse.

Stars that twinkle, nights so clear,
Echoes of the times we cheer.
In the silence, joy ignites,
Radiant waves on starlit nights.

With every glance, a spark ignites,
In the dark, our love ignites.
Together we weave the light,
In our hearts, forever bright.

Beyond the Glimmer

In twilight's glow, the shadows dance,
A fleeting glance, a whispered chance.
Dreams arise like misty streams,
Carrying hope on silver beams.

Mountains high with snow-capped peaks,
Nature's wonders quietly speak.
Beyond the glimmer, pathways lead,
In every step, our hearts are freed.

Winds of change, they softly sigh,
The world awakes, and so do I.
Together, we will find the way,
Through every night and every day.

Stars align in cosmic dance,
Guiding us with their romance.
Hold my hand, let passions soar,
Beyond the glimmer, we explore.

In the depths of endless night,
We search for dreams, we chase the light.
Beyond horizons, stories bloom,
In every shadow, we find room.

Echoes from the Abyss

Deep within the silent sea,
Echoes call, remember me.
Waves of time, they rise and fall,
Whispers low, a distant call.

In the depths where shadows play,
Secrets linger, fade away.
Voices soft in veils of mist,
Memories that long persist.

Through the dark, a light will spark,
Guiding souls from `beyond the arc.
Tides will shift, but still we'll stay,
Bound by night, we find our way.

In the silence, truths are laid,
Haunting dreams will not evade.
Every heartbeat a refrain,
Echoes of love, joy, and pain.

Rising up, like mist at dawn,
From the depths, we are reborn.
In the echoes, we will find,
Peaceful waters calm the mind.

Shards of Silence

In the quiet, whispers break,
Shards of silence, hearts will ache.
Dreams collide in heavy air,
Fleeting moments spark our care.

Fingers brush on empty space,
Memories etched, a gentle trace.
Every pause, a story told,
In the silence, we grow bold.

Through the void, a voice will rise,
Offering hope, beneath the skies.
Fragments glint like broken glass,
Reflections dance, but do not pass.

In the shadows, comfort lies,
Healing words, soft lullabies.
Each shard placed with tender hands,
Crafted dreams from silent sands.

In the stillness, worlds align,
Every silence, a design.
Capturing moments soft and sweet,
Building bridges where hearts meet.

Luminescent Reverberations

In the night, stars softly gleam,
Whispers of light, a cosmic dream.
Moonlight dances on the tide,
Echoes of warmth, where hopes reside.

Crickets sing a lullaby,
Underneath the velvet sky.
Fireflies pulse with gentle glow,
Illuminating paths below.

Shadows drift, a fleeting trace,
In the stillness, we find grace.
Each heartbeat, a glowing thread,
Connecting all that's left unsaid.

Silent moments, breath held tight,
In this glow, we find our light.
Reverberations softly sway,
As dreams weave through the night and play.

Endless echoes, bright and free,
A symphony of destiny.
Holding magic in the night,
Together, we embrace the light.

Frosted Harmonies

Silent whispers, winter's breath,
Blanket soft, it hides beneath.
Snowflakes dance in frosty air,
Crafting dreams beyond compare.

Icicles hang, a crystal choir,
Glinting gold in sunset fire.
Trees adorned with nature's lace,
Each branch sparkles, a fine embrace.

Chill of night, a silent muse,
Nature's art, a subtle ruse.
Footsteps crunch on frozen ground,
In this peace, sweet solace found.

Luminous moon, a watchful eye,
Guiding hearts as time drifts by.
Frosted harmonies in tune,
Underneath the silver moon.

Gentle sighs of winter's song,
In this stillness, we belong.
Ember hearts in cloak of white,
We find warmth in frosty night.

Shimmering Shadows

Beneath the trees where whispers play,
Shadows dance at close of day.
Flickering lights, a secret sway,
In twilight's grasp, they softly stay.

Moonlit paths where dreams collide,
In the hush where secrets hide.
Echoes of laughter fill the air,
Shimmering shadows everywhere.

Leaves rustle as stories call,
Woven tales, both grand and small.
Every flicker, a tale untold,
In quiet whispers, the past unfolds.

Hearts entwined in the night's embrace,
Finding warmth in a magic place.
Guided by the stars above,
Shimmering shadows teach us love.

In the dark, we lose our fear,
With shimmering shadows drawing near.
Together we breathe in the light,
In the beauty of the night.

The Sound of Glass

A fragile world, it holds its breath,
In the stillness, whispers death.
Echoing notes of brittle chime,
Moments frozen, lost in time.

Reflections dance on surfaces bright,
Capturing dreams, a fleeting light.
Crystals shatter, sharp and clear,
Each splinter sings of hope and fear.

There's beauty found in fragile things,
In every crack, a story sings.
Glistening shards in the twilight glow,
Carving silence, soft and slow.

Tremors echo in gentle sound,
A symphony of lost and found.
In this space, we find our way,
The sound of glass, a bright ballet.

Cradle the moments, hold them near,
In glassy whispers, life feels clear.
Each note, a heartbeat, soft and fast,
The sound of glass, a spell to last.

Alabaster Serenades

In the still of night, whispers play,
Soft echoes of dreams, drifting away.
Moonlight weaves through silver trees,
Cradling secrets in a tender breeze.

Stars twinkle low, a velvet sigh,
Painting the darkness, a lullaby.
Alabaster glow on tranquil streams,
Awakening the heart's hidden dreams.

Every shadow dances, light entwined,
Glows of peace in the night's unwind.
Hushed moments linger, a sacred pause,
Embracing beauty, in gentle cause.

The world transforms in this serene space,
A canvas of wonder, time's embrace.
Where silence blooms, and whispers flow,
Alabaster serenades, soft and slow.

The Dance of Light

A gentle shimmer on the morning dew,
The sun ascends, painting skies anew.
Golden rays waltz in a warm embrace,
Illuminating shadows, grace upon grace.

Through branches swaying, whispers glide,
In the dance of light, all worries slide.
Nature hums a vibrant refrain,
Each heartbeat echoes, joy unchained.

Colors burst forth in joyful cheer,
Painting the day with love sincere.
In every flicker, hope takes flight,
In the sacred art of the dance of light.

As twilight falls, hues softly blend,
Starlit paths where dreams transcend.
Embracing the night, we find our way,
In the echoes of light, forever stay.

Chords of the Glacier

Frozen echoes in the mountain's spine,
Whispers of time, eternal design.
Majestic silence, deep and profound,
Chords of the glacier in stillness found.

Each crystal shard gleams under the sun,
Capturing moments, each one by one.
Nature’s orchestra, each note reveals,
The harmony where the earth gently heals.

Rivers of ice flow, a timeless thread,
Carving through ages where legends tread.
In the heart of the cold, warmth resides,
Chords of the glacier, where peace abides.

As twilight descends on the icy crest,
Colors of dusk in the east manifest.
A serenade held in frozen grace,
Chords of the glacier, a sacred space.

Gleaming Traces

Footprints in sand, a fleeting trace,
Memories linger, time cannot erase.
Waves wash over, secrets unfold,
Gleaming traces in stories told.

Under the stars, connections flare,
Each twinkle a promise, a silent prayer.
Paths intertwine in the moonlight's glow,
Tracing the journeys where hearts will go.

Letters of love written in the sky,
Gleaming traces where dreams fly high.
Every heartbeat leaves a mark,
In the tapestry woven, eternal spark.

The sun sets low, painting the sea,
Echoes of laughter, wild and free.
As twilight deepens, we softly embrace,
Gleaming traces, a timeless grace.

Crystals in the Moonlight

Underneath the silver glow,
Crystals hum a tune so low.
Shimmering in tranquil grace,
Whispering dreams in their embrace.

Stars dance lightly in the sky,
While shadows weave and softly lie.
Moonlight kisses every stone,
Each reflecting truths unknown.

Gentle whispers fill the air,
Awakening the night’s sweet care.
Crystals twinkle, hopes anew,
Guided by the night’s soft hue.

In the dark, their secrets shine,
Patterns formed by fate divine.
A tapestry of wonder here,
Crafted by the night’s sincere.

Every shard, a story told,
Of lives once lived, of hearts of gold.
Embraced by night, forever bright,
Crystals gleam in moon’s soft light.

Harmonies of Dusk

When day gives way to evening’s sigh,
A symphony where shadows lie.
Colors blend in soft reprise,
As twilight wraps the earth’s disguise.

Birds return to nest and rest,
In gentle hues, they find their best.
The sky adorned in purple’s grace,
Time lingers in this sacred space.

Whispers float on evening’s breeze,
Nature sings, it aims to please.
Each leaf and branch in harmony,
Joining the dusk's sweet melody.

Stars awaken, one by one,
As daylight’s work is finally done.
Night invites the dreams to play,
A canvas where the heart can sway.

Moments pause in amber light,
A promise whispered, pure delight.
In dusk's embrace, the world transforms,
As peace is found in quiet storms.

Radiance in the Void

In the silence of the night,
Stars emerge, a guiding light.
Through the vast and endless dark,
Hope ignites a tiny spark.

Galaxies whirl in cosmic dance,
Infinite, as if by chance.
Whispers travel through the time,
Echoing in rhythms sublime.

Veils of night, so deep and wide,
Hold the dreams we seek to hide.
Yet in shadows, truth will bloom,
Radiance dispels the gloom.

Celestial hymns resonate,
Speaking softly of our fate.
The void, a canvas broad and free,
Painting visions yet to see.

In the depths of endless space,
Lies a beauty full of grace.
Within the dark, the light will find,
Infinite treasures for the mind.

The Language of Light

Words unspoken fill the air,
Illuminated by a flare.
Each ray, a note of soft refrain,
In every shadow, joy and pain.

Morning breaks with hues so bright,
Painting dreams in pure delight.
Every glimmer, a tale to share,
In the silence, we all care.

A sunbeam's touch, a gentle kiss,
Filling hearts with warmth and bliss.
Light cascades like whispered song,
Binding all the right and wrong.

Reflections dance upon the sea,
Speaking truths we long to be.
In every sparkle, hope ignites,
A reminder of our inner sights.

The language flows from dawn to dusk,
In every moment, love's deep trust.
Through light, we find our way to heal,
Filling the void with what we feel.

Lightwaves and Reveries

In the morning glow we rise,
Tracing dreams across the skies.
Whispers soft as dawn's embrace,
Kisses of light in a gentle race.

Colors dance in a silver stream,
Awakening the heart's deep seam.
Radiant paths through shadows chase,
Guided by hope's eternal face.

Waves of amber, golden hue,
Carrying wishes born anew.
Every ray, a story told,
In the warmth, the world unfolds.

Moments flicker, time stands still,
The air is charged with a vibrant thrill.
Light reveals what's lost, then found,
In reveries, our souls abound.

As dusk descends, we hold the spark,
A tapestry woven, bright and dark.
In every glimmer, a path we trace,
Lightwaves dance in sacred space.

The Geometry of Silence

In shadows deep, the echoes lie,
A language felt, yet never shy.
Angles sharp in the quiet night,
Where thoughts collide, but not in sight.

Shapes of peace weave through the air,
Fractals of calm in stillness bare.
Each pause a corner, each breath a line,
In the silence, whispers align.

Time bends softly on the edge,
Moments paused, a quiet pledge.
Points of view shift in the dark,
Illuminating paths we embark.

Finding meaning in vacant space,
Amidst the void, a warm embrace.
Geometry of hearts laid bare,
In the silence, we find our share.

Ciphers written in hushed tones,
Resonant depths in muted zones.
Within the quiet, secrets dwell,
In the geometry, we find our spell.

Ethereal Fragments

Scattered glimmers in twilight's grace,
Whispers of dreams, we all can trace.
Echos linger, soft and bright,
In the stillness, we take flight.

Shattered stars in a velvet sea,
All the pieces that once were free.
Fragments dance on a fleeting breeze,
Whirling thoughts, a gentle tease.

Threads of silver, shadows play,
In every angle, memories sway.
Capturing laughter, holding tears,
Crafting tales across the years.

Breath of night, unseen, unbound,
Ethereal whispers swirl around.
In the echoes, we find our thread,
Rest in the places dreams have led.

Fleeting joy, a soft refrain,
Stitching together the pleasure and pain.
In fragments, beauty finds its song,
In each piece, where we all belong.

Ribbons of Ice

Crystal tendrils in winter’s grasp,
Mirroring dreams we choose to clasp.
Delicate forms, a shivering art,
In ribbons of ice, we find our heart.

Glacial whispers, secrets shared,
In frosted lines, the world prepared.
Each breath of chill a canvas bright,
In the quiet, we lose our fright.

Shadows cast in azure hue,
Painting pathways, cold but true.
Nature’s brush in softest strokes,
In ribbons of ice, the heart evokes.

Fleeting moments caught in time,
Frosted beauty, a silent rhyme.
Echoes resonate from below,
In winter's hold, our spirits grow.

With every thaw, a tale unveils,
In the melting, we trace our trails.
Ribbons of ice forever will blend,
In the cycle that never ends.

Frosty Rhythms

In the cradle of winter's chill,
Snowflakes dance on the windowsill.
Whispers of frost, soft and bright,
Nature's lullaby in the silent night.

Trees wear gowns of sparkling white,
Moonbeams cast a silver light.
Footsteps crunch on the frozen ground,
In this stillness, peace is found.

The air hangs crisp, a breath of cold,
As stories of winter gently unfold.
Stars twinkle above in the deep blue,
Echoes of dreams that feel so true.

Embers glow in the hearth’s embrace,
Warmth that counters the frosty space.
Together we gather, hearts aligned,
In these rhythms, our souls entwined.

The Mirror's Song

Reflections dance in polished glass,
Fragments of time that come to pass.
Faces change, yet truth remains,
In the depths, glory and pains.

Whispers carried on gentle waves,
The mirror holds the stories it saves.
Eyes that twinkle, secrets shared,
Within its gaze, we are laid bare.

Each moment caught in silent frame,
Echoes of joy, shadows of shame.
A canvas where our lives collide,
In this stillness, we cannot hide.

Turn away, yet still it calls,
In the silence, destiny falls.
A song of truth, forever strong,
In the reflection, we find our song.

Ether of Transparency

In the ether, where thoughts align,
Visions blend, connections divine.
Veils of silence, whispers fly,
In clarity, the spirits sigh.

Truth unfolds like a fragile leaf,
In the light, we shed our grief.
Moments captured in gentle light,
Unraveling shadows, bidding goodnight.

Each heartbeat sounds a melody,
In transparency, we seek to be free.
A tapestry woven of dreams anew,
In this realm, we journey through.

Floating softly in endless space,
Finding solace in every trace.
Together we wander, spirits bold,
In the ether, stories told.

Celestial Shards

Stars scatter like shards of glass,
In the cosmos, they shimmer and pass.
Constellations tell tales of old,
Of adventures and dreams, brave and bold.

Each twinkle ignites a hidden flame,
In the night sky, we call their name.
Galaxies spin in a silent dance,
In their beauty, we take a chance.

Fleeting moments of stardust bliss,
Where wishes are made and dreams kiss.
The universe hums an ancient song,
In its depths, we all belong.

Cosmic echoes that never fade,
In the heart of night, wonders are laid.
Celestial shards in the dark remind,
Of the vastness that lies in the mind.

Undercurrents of Light

In whispers soft, the shadows play,
Beneath the sun, where dreams sway.
A flicker here, a glimmer there,
Secrets weave through thin air.

Rays of hope in twilight's grasp,
Glimpse of joy, a fleeting clasp.
Through gentle tides of warm embrace,
Light reveals a hidden space.

Echoes dance on waves of gold,
Stories waiting to be told.
In the depth, where silence dwells,
Undercurrents weave their spells.

A canvas bright, where dark meets light,
Shattering shadows, taking flight.
Hearts ignite with fire's glow,
In the dark, the bright seeds grow.

So linger here in twilight's weave,
Find the threads that we believe.
Eternity in moments caught,
In undercurrents, truth is sought.

Vibrations of Stillness

In the hush, the world can be,
A quiet place, a harmony.
Between the beats, there's life anew,
The pulse of peace, a gentle cue.

Whispers float on tranquil air,
Echoes of a mindful prayer.
Each heartbeat sings a subtle note,
In stillness, dreams begin to float.

Beneath the surface, ripples flow,
Embracing calm, letting go.
In silken threads of fading light,
Life vibrates with pure delight.

Trees listen to the silent song,
In stillness, where we all belong.
Nature breathes a quiet tune,
In this space, hearts become in tune.

So take a breath, let worries cease,
In the silence, find your peace.
Vibrations rise and softly stir,
In stillness, life begins to blur.

Shining Through the Veil

Behind the curtain of night’s cloak,
Stars whisper secrets, softly spoke.
In shadows deep, a light will gleam,
Shining brightly like a dream.

Through the haze of doubts and fears,
Hope appears, dispelling tears.
A silver thread, a guiding light,
Illuminates the darkest night.

Moments glisten, glowing bright,
Fragile as the dawn's first light.
With each shimmer, stories bloom,
Barriers fade, banishing gloom.

Across the divide, the souls connect,
In their spark, we find respect.
Vibrations of love, woven tight,
Shining through the mystic night.

So chase the stars with hearts ablaze,
In every shadow, find the rays.
For in the veil, truth’s light prevails,
Unity sings as love unveils.

Corners of the Mind

In hushed corners where thoughts collide,
Memories drift like a silent tide.
Echoes linger, whispering low,
In the depths where silence grows.

Fleeting visions, shadows dance,
Within the stillness, take a chance.
Wander through each hidden nook,
In the silence, learn to look.

Dreams unfold in fragile hues,
A tapestry of crimson blues.
Unraveled thoughts, like threads unwind,
Exploring the corners of the mind.

In twilight’s glow, where secrets rest,
Find the pieces that feel like the best.
Lost in reflections, we often find,
The beautiful chaos of the mind.

So come, explore the quiet maze,
In each corner, life conveys.
For in the mind's vast, winding road,
The heart sows the dreams, seeds bestowed.

Serene Chandeliers

In twilight's soft embrace they glow,
Glistening jewels hung low.
Whispers of light dance and sway,
Guiding dreams at end of day.

Crystals catch the fading sun,
Memories of laughter spun.
Each flicker tells a story old,
In their warmth, the heart is sold.

Glimmers spark in gentle grace,
A sanctuary, a sacred space.
Ethereal beauty fills the air,
A tranquil charm beyond compare.

Reflections play on polished floors,
Softly echoing love's sweet roars.
A moment caught in time's embrace,
Serenity found in this place.

Beneath the glow, worries cease,
In the light, we find our peace.
With every shimmer, hope ignites,
In the serenity of lights.

Echoing Delights

In the forest, laughter rings,
As birds weave songs on golden wings.
Footsteps fall on mossy ground,
Every echo, joy profound.

Sunbeams filter through the leaves,
Whispers that the heart believes.
Nature's orchestra plays its tune,
A symphony beneath the moon.

Rustling leaves, a gentle sigh,
In the quiet, dreams will fly.
The world unfolds with each heartbeat,
In every moment, life feels sweet.

Mountains cradle secrets old,
Echoing stories yet untold.
The river flows with whispers bright,
Illuminating day and night.

Together we chase fleeting sounds,
In every note, love abounds.
These echoes dance, a fleeting flight,
Creating magic, pure delight.

Illumined Thoughts

In the quiet of the night,
Stars ignite our hearts with light.
Each glimmer sparks a wandering mind,
Illumined dreams we seek to find.

Amidst the silence, visions flare,
Thoughts lifted high, floating in air.
Ideas bloom like flowers bright,
In the realm of endless light.

Whispers weave through cosmic streams,
Filling the void with vibrant dreams.
Every heartbeat sings its song,
In this dance, we all belong.

A tapestry of thoughts unfurl,
Connecting hearts across the world.
Through light of night, our spirits soar,
Illuminated evermore.

The dawn will chase the stars away,
Yet in our minds, they'll always stay.
Illumined thoughts, a guiding force,
Lighting up our destined course.

Silvery Reverberations

In moonlight's glow, the night awakes,
Gentle tides in rhythm shakes.
Soft whispers ride the silver waves,
Carrying secrets time engraves.

Echoes dance on tranquil shores,
Each melody, a heart restores.
In the stillness, magic flows,
Luminous love forever glows.

Stars twinkle in the velvet sky,
Filling dreams as they pass by.
In the silence, we draw near,
Listening close, the world we hear.

Harmonies of night enthrall,
As shadows play on ancient wall.
In every reverberation bright,
We find our way back to the light.

Forever bound by cosmic fate,
We trace the paths that love creates.
With every echo, hearts align,
In silvery threads, our souls entwine.

The Echoing Silence

In shadows deep, the whispers play,
A melody lost, drifting away.
Thoughts woven tight, yet fragile as lace,
In this quiet void, I find my place.

A heartbeat sounds, a distant call,
Resonating softly through the hall.
Every breath taken, an echo resists,
In the stillness, the world exists.

The clock ticks slow, a haunting sound,
Its rhythm shapes the thoughts unbound.
Each moment lingers, suspended in air,
A dance with silence, beyond compare.

The shadows stretch, pulling me near,
In the absence of words, I hear.
Infinite stories wrapped deep inside,
In the echoing silence, I confide.

A symphony played on strings so thin,
The quiet speaks louder than where I've been.
In the heart of the calm, I dare to believe,
The echoes of silence, my soul's reprieve.

Glistening Mosaics

Fragments of color, scattered and bright,
Reflecting the world in beams of light.
Shattered dreams form a splendid display,
Glistening mosaics of joy and dismay.

Each piece, a story, a journey untold,
Crafted by time, and moments unfold.
Rays of the sun kiss the glassy seams,
Together they whisper both hope and dreams.

In the quiet of dusk, as shadows grow long,
These tiny reflections weave a new song.
Nature's own canvas, a tapestry wide,
In its vibrant colors, we learn to abide.

The echoes of laughter, the sighs of the heart,
In this mosaic, we each play our part.
Every break, a memory, every hue,
A testament to life, vibrant and true.

With each gentle breeze, a shimmer ignites,
Bringing forth visions of magical sights.
In this dance of colors, we find our place,
Glistening mosaics in time's embrace.

Threads of Radiance

Fine strands of gold weave through the night,
Illuminating dreams, casting pure light.
Whispers of hope in the fabric of fate,
Threads of radiance that twinkle and sate.

In the tapestry spun, our stories entwine,
Each moment a stitch, a heartbeat divine.
Through shadows we wander, seeking the glow,
Guided by threads only few ever know.

Each shimmer holds secrets, both vast and deep,
Links of existence where memories seep.
Woven together, horizons expand,
In the threads of radiance, we take our stand.

A dance of the galaxies spins in the dark,
Each thread a connection, igniting the spark.
With every heartbeat, the fabric grows strong,
Threads of radiance sing our own song.

In the quiet of dawn, as the stars fade away,
The threads of our lives guide the dawn's ray.
Forever we'll flourish, in light we'll advance,
Through the threads of radiance, we find our dance.

Soundscapes in Glacial Time

Whispers of glaciers drift through the night,
Soundscapes moving, a gentle delight.
Each crack and creak, a tale to unfold,
In the rhythm of ice, a story retold.

Time slows its march in this frozen embrace,
Eons compressed in this tranquil space.
A symphony born from the still and the cold,
Nature's own chorus, both tender and bold.

The echoes of water trickle and flow,
In silence they linger, deep down below.
A language of crystals, of frost and of light,
Creating a canvas both wild and bright.

With each grain of snow, a melody formed,
In this landscape vast, both peaceful and warmed.
The heartbeat of glaciers, slow yet profound,
In soundscapes of time, our solace is found.

Through ages of ice, a beauty persists,
The music of nature in gentle twists.
In the stillness we gather, our spirits align,
In soundscapes of peace, we find our design.

Echoes from the Depths

In shadows deep where secrets lie,
Whispers of the past float by.
Silent echoes in the night,
Fleeting glimpses, soft and bright.

Memories dance upon the wave,
Calling to the hearts so brave.
In the silence, stories blend,
Where the ocean's tales descend.

With every tide, they rise and fall,
The haunting calls of the ocean's thrall.
Painting pictures in the breeze,
Eternal echoes, never cease.

From the depths, a voice rings clear,
A melody that draws us near.
In the gloom, there’s light and song,
An ancient tale where we belong.

In the waters, wisdom flows,
An endless cycle, life bestows.
Listen close, let fears take flight,
Embrace the depths, find your light.

Ethereality in Ice

Frozen breath of winter's kiss,
In the stillness, find your bliss.
Each crystal spark a fleeting dream,
Caught within a silver seam.

Glistening paths under moon's glow,
Shadows dance where cold winds blow.
Silence wraps the world in white,
Holding secrets, pure and bright.

Glass-like surfaces, smooth and clear,
A fragile beauty, drawing near.
In each flake, a story told,
Of fleeting warmth in the cold.

Softly whispers through the trees,
The heartbeat of the winter breeze.
Ethereal dreams take their flight,
In the embrace of peaceful night.

Every spark a moment’s grace,
Nature's canvas, time's embrace.
In this stillness, life will wait,
In the magic, we create.

Glints of Memory

Faded snapshots in the mind,
Joys and sorrows intertwined.
Moments glimmer, soft and rare,
Echoes linger in the air.

Time's embrace holds all that's dear,
Silent stories, crystal clear.
In the heart, where treasures lie,
Whispers of those days gone by.

Every laugh, each tear we shed,
A tapestry of life we've led.
Through the corridors of time,
Memories dance, a silent rhyme.

Though the years may drift away,
In our hearts, they choose to stay.
Glimmers of what we once knew,
Painted skies in every hue.

In the twilight, thoughts will roam,
Finding solace, coming home.
Every glint, a light to share,
Reminders of love’s gentle care.

The Refined Chime

In the stillness, bells will ring,
Echoes of a song they bring.
Soft and clear, a soothing sound,
In their melody, peace is found.

Carried on the whispering breeze,
Notes colliding with the trees.
Joyful laughter fills the air,
In the rhythm, life lays bare.

Crafted by the hands of time,
Every chime a perfect rhyme.
Transcendent, pure, and deeply true,
Each moment sings, just like you.

Listen close to nature's choir,
Harmonies that lift us higher.
In the echoes, dreams align,
Magic hides in every line.

With each note, the heart will dance,
Lost in music's sweet expanse.
Let the refined chime guide your way,
In this symphony, forever stay.

Dreaming in Tints

In shades of blue, the skies unfold,
Whispers of dreams in stories told.
A canvas vast, where thoughts can roam,
Painting the heart, we find our home.

With strokes of gold and hints of green,
Visions dance in a playful sheen.
Clouds drift softly, colors blend,
In this dreamscape, time can bend.

Each hue a feeling, each shade a song,
Guiding the heart where we belong.
Mirrored echoes in twilight's glow,
In this enchanted land, we flow.

As starlit whispers grace the night,
Colors of dreams take wondrous flight.
In the silence, our spirits entwine,
Carried by hues, both yours and mine.

Through every tint, a tale is spun,
Of laughter, love, and days undone.
In this realm where visions gleam,
We chase the vibrant threads of dream.

Murmurs of the Unknown

In shadows deep, the secrets lie,
Echoes whisper, soft as a sigh.
Threads of silence weave through the night,
Murmurs beckon, lost in the light.

Beneath the stars, a hidden path,
Where mysteries linger, feel their wrath.
Voices call from ages past,
In the stillness, shadows cast.

These murmurs swirl, like leaves in wind,
Stories of journeys, hearts rescind.
Unearth the tales, let them unfold,
In the darkness, the truth is bold.

Each whisper carries a gentle plea,
Unlock the chains, set spirits free.
In realms where light and dark collide,
The unknown beckons, our hearts abide.

With every breath, we seek to find,
What lies beyond, what's intertwined.
In the echoes, we hear our name,
Murmurs of fate, an endless game.

Spheres of Reflection

In still waters, secrets gleam,
Mirrored worlds in a gentle dream.
Spheres of thought twist and turn,
Within their depths, passions burn.

Gazing deep into the glass,
Time stands still, moments pass.
Reflections of what's yet to be,
Circular paths set our spirits free.

Each circle holds a tale untold,
Of laughter shared and hearts of gold.
In the silence, lessons learned,
Through every sphere, we've gently turned.

What lies within the twist of fate?
Each layer peeled, we contemplate.
In rippling echoes, we find our fight,
In every sphere, a spark ignites.

Cradle the visions, let them flow,
In spheres of reflection, we come to know.
What lies beyond, what's pure, what's real,
In every glance, we start to heal.

Twilight's Chime

As day gives way to night's embrace,
Twilight whispers, a gentle grace.
In soft hues, the world aligns,
Time pauses here, as twilight shines.

Each curve of light, a dance of dreams,
Echoes linger, or so it seems.
Pastel skies and shadows play,
In twilight's chime, we drift away.

Silhouettes stretch against the glow,
In the calm, our spirits flow.
Beauty cradles the fading light,
In murmurs soft, we find our flight.

The horizon blushes, stars ignite,
Painting the canvas of the night.
With every chime, a promise waits,
In twilight's arms, love resonates.

We breathe in magic, rich and deep,
In this twilight, our souls leap.
With every sigh, we feel the breeze,
Charmed by twilight, we find our ease.

Seraphic Echoes

In the hush of twilight's glow,
Angels whisper secrets low.
Wings unfurl, the stars align,
Echoes soft, divine, benign.

Through the veil of dreams we tread,
Light and shadow gently wed.
In the silence, hearts can soar,
Seraphic songs forevermore.

In the garden of the night,
Hope ignites a flickering light.
Celestial voices intertwine,
Guiding souls through realms divine.

Boundless skies our spirits chase,
Lost in love, we find our place.
As the stars begin to fade,
In echoes sweet, our dreams are made.

Where horizons kiss the sky,
In the stillness, time will fly.
Seraphic echoes, pure and bright,
Guide us softly to the light.

Melodies of Clarity

In the morning's gentle glow,
Whispers dance, and feelings flow.
Notes of truth in every breeze,
Set our troubled minds at ease.

With each chord, our hearts align,
Melodies of love divine.
Through the chaos, find your way,
Clarity in every sway.

Harmony in every breath,
Life embraced, defying death.
With each song, the soul will rise,
Revealing beauty in disguise.

In the stillness of the night,
Melodies take lofty flight.
Echoes of forgotten dreams,
Flow like gentle, silver streams.

Let the music guide your hands,
Crafting hope in shifting sands.
In unity, we shall stand,
Singing songs across the land.

Find the rhythm deep within,
Let the journey now begin.
With each note, the world will see,
Melodies of clarity.

A Dance with the Ethereal

In twilight's veil, we find our chance,
To step beneath the moonlit trance.
Hands entwined, we spin and sway,
In harmony, we drift away.

Past the shadows, spirits call,
Whispers soft, we break the fall.
With every step, we come alive,
In this dance, our souls arrive.

Through cosmic realms and skies we'll glide,
With the stars as our guide.
In the rhythm, time stands still,
As dreams collide with sheer will.

Let the ethereal winds embrace,
Every turn, each woven space.
In the still, we lose our fears,
And dance away our silent tears.

Floating gently through the night,
With every heartbeat, pure delight.
In this celestial masquerade,
Our spirits dance where love cascades.

Awakened hearts now soar and fly,
In unity, we touch the sky.
In this dance, forever twirl,
A love entwined, a shining pearl.

Frostbitten Harmonies

In winter's grasp, we hold our breath,
A chill that speaks of life and death.
Through icy veils, the melodies weave,
Echoes clad in frost, we believe.

Silent whispers in the snow,
Guide the way for those who know.
Each flake a tale, a song unsung,
In frozen realms, our hearts are strung.

Amidst the white, a warmth ignites,
Frostbitten harmonies take flight.
As laughter dances in the air,
Joy emerges, pure and rare.

With every note, the hearth's alive,
In the cold, our spirits thrive.
Nature's chorus fills the night,
In icy shadows, love shines bright.

Through stark beauty, we will find,
A symphony that transcends time.
In winter's heart, we find our tune,
Frostbitten dreams beneath the moon.

So take my hand, together we'll roam,
In the chill, we create our home.
In harmony, we face the storm,
Frostbitten love, forever warm.

Luminescent Reflections

Beneath the stars, the waters glow,
Mirroring dreams from long ago.
Whispers dance on gentle waves,
Secrets hidden, a heart that craves.

In twilight's brush, colors blend,
A canvas where the shadows mend.
Each flicker tells a tale anew,
Of hopes once lost, now shining through.

The moon casts light on silver shores,
As night unfolds and softly roars.
With every breath, the night expands,
Infinite wonders in its hands.

Reflections call the spirit near,
Echoing a voice we hold dear.
In stillness found, the world ignites,
A symphony of silent nights.

As dawn approaches, colors fade,
Yet in the heart, the light is laid.
For every star that leaves the sky,
Will find a way to always fly.

Echoes in the Ice

Crystalline whispers fill the air,
Frozen tales of dark and rare.
Each creak and groan tells ancient lore,
In timeless frost, the spirits soar.

Shadows linger in a misty trance,
Dancing on the surface, a fleeting chance.
Every shard reflects a face,
Of moments locked in cold embrace.

Beneath the surface, secrets sleep,
Silent echoes, profound and deep.
Glimmers sparkle in the harshest night,
Remnants of warmth, a soft delight.

Voices call from ages gone,
In the stillness, we feel the dawn.
Each breath a promise, crisp and clear,
In frozen realms, the truth draws near.

Yet beauty thrives in chilly breath,
Life endures through silent death.
In icy realms, all things align,
Where echoes dwell and hearts entwine.

Beauty in Fractals

In patterns woven, nature's grace,
Infinite forms in every space.
Each curve and twist, a story spun,
In fractals bright, we see the sun.

Mighty forests breathe in sync,
Leaves unfurl, without a blink.
Mountains rise in mirrored arrays,
Reflecting life in myriad ways.

Snowflakes fall in perfect art,
Dancing down with joyful heart.
Unique designs in every flake,
Nature's brush, no move to fake.

Rivers wind like dreams anew,
Creating paths that greet the blue.
In every drop, a universe,
A song of life, profound, diverse.

Beauty blooms in chaos pure,
In every shape, of this I'm sure.
Fractals show us how to see,
The wonders in our tapestry.

Ghostly Glimmers

In twilight's veil, the spirits tread,
Whispers brush past where shadows spread.
Flickering lights in the darkened woods,
Echo the tales of misunderstood.

Glimmers dance on a haunted breeze,
Entwined with sighs from ancient trees.
Every flick reveals a trace,
Of every soul, a fleeting face.

In silver mist, their stories flow,
Haunting the paths where lost hearts go.
Lost in time, yet always near,
A spectral realm devoid of fear.

These echoes twine around our fate,
In quiet moments, we contemplate.
What once was life, now softly gleams,
In spectral shadows, in our dreams.

A ghostly glow in the midnight hush,
Calls out to those who feel the rush.
With every heartbeat, we remember,
The light that flickers, a ghostly ember.

Ghosts of Radiance

In shadows where the whispers play,
Flickering lights begin to sway.
Gentle echoes from the past,
Ghosts of radiance that will last.

Hazy images drift and glide,
Memories in the evening tide.
Softly bathing in the glow,
Secrets only they can know.

Dancing amid the trees so tall,
Silhouettes that rise and fall.
Each beam of light softly speaks,
Of hidden paths and mystic peaks.

Through the night, their laughter flows,
Guiding where the starlight goes.
In this realm, the lost reside,
Ghosts of radiance, time's great tide.

A flicker here, a shimmer there,
In twilight's breath, a gentle air.
Weaving tales of love and fate,
Ghosts of radiance, never late.

The Prism's Lullaby

Colors dance on evening's cheek,
In every hue, a story speaks.
In twilight's arms, they intertwine,
The prism’s lullaby, so divine.

Soft currents in the fading light,
Carry dreams into the night.
A whisper of a gentle breeze,
Melodies that bring us ease.

Crimson, blue, and golden shades,
Create a world where hope cascades.
In silence, notes begin to soar,
The prism's lullaby, evermore.

Under stars with radiant grace,
The universe finds its place.
Swaying softly, shadows glide,
In the prism's lullaby, we hide.

As dawn breaks, the colors fade,
But in our hearts, they never stayed.
With every sunrise, memories bloom,
The prism's lullaby, our tune.

Whirlwinds of Clarity

In restless gusts, the thoughts collide,
Whirlwinds of clarity, a fierce tide.
Rushing through the mind's expanse,
Awakening dreams, igniting chance.

Promises twirl in the swirling air,
Each one shines, each one rare.
Lightning bolts of insight strike,
Whirlwinds of clarity, take hike.

Amidst the chaos, moments pause,
In the storm, we find a cause.
With every breath, we gain new sight,
Whirlwinds guiding us to light.

A dance to rhythms unseen,
Through the tempest, sleek and keen.
Embrace the winds, let them steer,
Whirlwinds of clarity, draw us near.

As calm descends, we find our way,
With clearer minds, we seize the day.
In every twist, a path revealed,
Whirlwinds of clarity, our shield.

Silent Symphony

In quiet halls, the echoes dwell,
A silent symphony to tell.
With every heartbeat, notes arise,
In stillness, music never dies.

Soft harmonies weave through the air,
A melody beyond compare.
In shadows' grip, emotions flow,
A silent symphony we know.

Each whispered note, a gentle sigh,
The universe's lullaby.
Through unseen realms, it travels far,
A silent symphony, like a star.

With tender grace, it cradles dreams,
In every silence, hope redeems.
In every heart, it finds its space,
A silent symphony, time's embrace.

As daylight fades, the music swells,
In every soul, its beauty dwells.
In quiet moments, let it play,
A silent symphony, here to stay.

The Fragility of Sound

Whispers drift in twilight air,
Softly breaking, unaware.
A gentle breeze holds tales of old,
In silence, secrets unfold.

Chimes of laughter, fleeting notes,
In echoes washed by time's own moats.
A lullaby of fading light,
Dispersed like stars in the night.

Rustling leaves, a hidden dance,
Nature's song in a fleeting chance.
The murmurs blend, a woven thread,
A symphony where all are led.

Footsteps fade on cobblestone,
Retreat to silence, all alone.
In every word, a world contained,
In quietude, all is gained.

Listen close, the fragile plea,
To hold the sound, to let it be.
For in the stillness, hearts will find,
The echoes of a gentle mind.

Luminary Glimmers

Stars awake in velvet skies,
Twinkling bright, where silence lies.
Guiding wanderers on their way,
Shimmering whispers, night to day.

Moonlit paths of silver sheen,
Painting dreams with gentle green.
In shadows deep, the light will play,
Leaving hints of hope's soft sway.

Glimmers dance on water's face,
A mirrored world, a timeless grace.
Each flicker tells a story sweet,
A symphony, life's heartbeat.

Fading flames in twilight's kiss,
Hold the promise of pure bliss.
Each moment shines, a fleeting trace,
In every glimmer, find your place.

Breathe the night, let starlight in,
Feel the magic deep within.
For every glimmer holds the key,
To unlock dreams, to set you free.

Echoing Fractals

In patterns vast, the worlds collide,
Infinite designs where thoughts abide.
Reflecting moments, shapes that blend,
A dance of echoes around the bend.

Fractals bloom in vibrant hues,
Each twist, a choice, in every muse.
From chaos emerges a tale untold,
In the heart of fractals, mysteries unfold.

Waves of sound in swirling grace,
Resonating in timeless space.
Each pulse, a map of who we are,
In echoes near and echoes far.

Life's labyrinth of depth and height,
Guides us through the shadowed night.
With every turn, learn to embrace,
The fractal dance, the endless chase.

Let the echoes weave your soul,
In their rhythm, find your whole.
For in the mirrored voice you hear,
Resides the truth, forever clear.

The Harmony of the Frost

Winter's breath, a gentle touch,
Whispers secrets, soft and hush.
Every crystal, a note that sings,
In fragile beauty, silence clings.

A tapestry of white so bright,
Framing moments in pure delight.
In the cold, warmth can be found,
In every flake, a love profound.

Trees adorned with frozen lace,
Nature's art in a quiet space.
Each branch holds a symphony,
Of chilly winds that roam so free.

As dawn breaks with a golden hue,
The frost will dance, a waltz anew.
In harmony, the world awakes,
From slumber, beauty softly breaks.

Feel the magic in the air,
In stillness, find the beauty rare.
For in the frost, a song is spun,
A winter's tale, for everyone.

Ethereal Reflections

In the stillness of the night,
Stars whisper secrets bright.
Moonlight dances on the lake,
Silent dreams begin to wake.

Glistening waves of silver hue,
Carrying thoughts that feel so true.
A breeze that gently sways the trees,
Echoing nature's softest pleas.

The nightingale sings its sweet song,
In this moment, we belong.
Reflections ripple in the dark,
Igniting every hidden spark.

Wisps of clouds float overhead,
Where ancient tales and spirits tread.
Each twinkle tells a story old,
In the silence, we are bold.

As dawn approaches with soft light,
The world transforms, a wondrous sight.
Yet in my heart, the night remains,
Eternal echoes in my veins.

Icicle Harmonies

Beneath the frost, the world lies still,
Icicles form on the windowsill.
Each drop of water, a crystal song,
Nature's symphony, pure and strong.

Winter winds weave tales so grand,
Of ancient times, a cold command.
Snowflakes twirl like dancers fair,
Frosty breath hangs in the air.

Branches bow with heavy white,
Glistening under the pale moonlight.
A hush envelops the sleeping ground,
In this serenity, peace is found.

A fire crackles, warmly glows,
Outside the tempest fiercely blows.
But within these walls, we find our grace,
In icicle harmonies, we embrace.

The chill may bite, the cold may sting,
Yet love ignites, our hearts take wing.
Until the thaw, we revel here,
In winter's grasp, we hold so dear.

Shimmering Shadows

In twilight's glow, the shadows play,
Whispering secrets of the day.
Sunset colors paint the skies,
A masterpiece that never lies.

Beneath their veil, a world unseen,
Where dreams reside in soft routine.
Every whisper, a gentle touch,
In the dark, we feel so much.

Silhouettes dance on the cathedral walls,
Echoing laughter, as twilight calls.
A flicker of hope, a flicker of fear,
In shimmering shadows, we draw near.

The night unfolds its velvet cloak,
Wrapped in silence, we softly spoke.
Stars emerge to weave their tale,
Guiding us through the night's frail veil.

As the moon rises, bold and bright,
Shadows blend with the soft twilight.
We wander lost, yet somehow found,
In the shimmering twilight, we're spellbound.

Celestial Resonance

Echoes of the cosmos soar,
Inviting us to explore.
Galaxies spin in endless flight,
Illuminating the velvet night.

Stars pulse with ancient lore,
Tales of love and dreams galore.
Underneath this cosmic dome,
We discover, we find our home.

Comets blaze a fiery trail,
In their wake, our hopes set sail.
Celestial whispers fill the void,
In this vastness, love's employed.

Planets dance in harmonious time,
Creating rhythms, a space sublime.
Every heartbeat, a note profound,
In celestial resonance, we are found.

With open hearts, we gaze above,
In the starlight, we feel love.
For in the heavens, we connect,
In cosmic dreams, we reflect.

Milton Keynes UK
Ingram Content Group UK Ltd.
UKHW021359081224
452111UK00007B/103

9 789916 799666